The
Ballad
of
William Bloat

Hector McDonnell, son of the 13th Earl of Antrim, was born in 1947. His educational career took him from Eton to Munich, Oxford, and to Vienna, where he studied sculpture under the leading Austrian sculptor Wotruba. His work has been exhibited in galleries in London, Belfast, Dublin, Paris, Brussels, Munich and Vienna. In 1979 he won an important German art competition, the Darmstädter Kunstpreis, and as a result of this had a major retrospective exhibition in the Matildenhöhe in Darmstadt the following year.

In 1982 he illustrated *Saturday Night in York Street,* a collection of poems by Belfast's docker poet, John Campbell.

He divides his time between his home in London and the family seat at Glenarm in County Antrim.

The original William Bloat etchings were produced in an edition of 25.

The
Ballad
of
William Bloat

a poem
by
Raymond Calvert

illustrated
by
Hector McDonnell

The
Blackstaff Press

These illustrations to
'The Ballad of William Bloat'
are dedicated to my dear cousin,
Doctor Honor Smith,
from whom I first heard this ballad,
and whose witty rendering of it
inspired me to make these drawings.

In a
mean abode
on the
Shankill Road

Lived a man
called
William Bloat.

He had
a
wife,
the curse
of his
life,

*Who
continually
got his
goat.*

*So
one day
at dawn,
with
her nightdress
on,
he cut
her
bloody throat.*

With
a razor gash
he settled
her hash,
Oh never
was crime
so quick,
but
the steady drip
on the
pillow slip
of her
lifeblood
made him
sick,

And
the pool of gore
on the
bedroom floor
grew
clotted cold
and
thick.

And
yet he was glad
that he'd
done
what he had,
when she lay there
stiff and still,
but
a sudden awe
of the
angry law
struck his soul
with
an icy chill.

*So
to finish the fun
so well begun,
he resolved
himself
to kill.*

Then
he took the sheet
off his wife's
cold feet,
and
twisted it
into a rope,

And
he hanged himself
from
the pantry shelf.
'Twas an easy end,
let's hope.
In
the face of death
with his
latest breath,
he solemnly
cursed
the Pope.

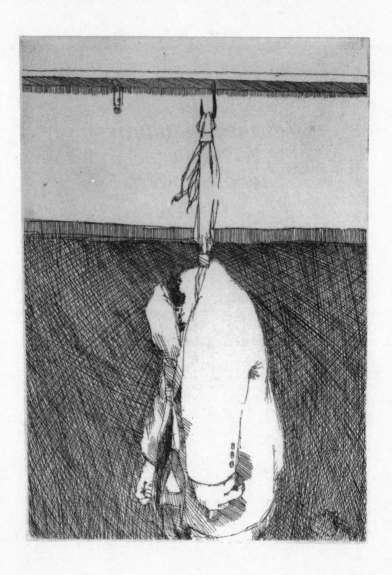

*But
the strangest turn
to the
whole concern
is only
just beginnin'.*

*He went to Hell
but
his wife got well,
and
she's still alive
and sinnin',*

*For
the razor blade
was
foreign made,
but
the sheet
was
Irish linen.*

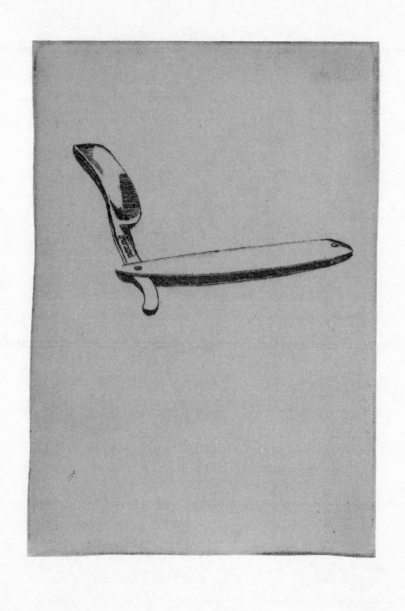

THE BALLAD
OF
WILLIAM BLOAT

In a mean abode on the Shankill Road
Lived a man called William Bloat.
He had a wife, the curse of his life,
Who continually got his goat.
So one day at dawn, with her nightdress on,
He cut her bloody throat.

With a razor gash he settled her hash,
Oh never was crime so quick,
But the steady drip on the pillow slip
Of her lifeblood made him sick,
And the pool of gore on the bedroom floor
Grew clotted cold and thick.

And yet he was glad that he'd done what he had,
When she lay there stiff and still,
But a sudden awe of the angry law
Struck his soul with an icy chill.
So to finish the fun so well begun,
He resolved himself to kill.

Then he took the sheet off his wife's cold feet,
And twisted it into a rope,
And he hanged himself from the pantry shelf.
'Twas an easy end, let's hope.
In the face of death with his latest breath,
He solemnly cursed the Pope.

But the strangest turn to the whole concern
Is only just beginnin'.
He went to Hell but his wife got well,
And she's still alive and sinnin',
For the razor blade was foreign made,
But the sheet was Irish linen.

Raymond Colville Calvert was born at Banchory House, Helen's Bay, County of Down, on 30 October 1906 and died there on 11 July 1959. He was the only son and younger child of William Henderson Calvert, a well-known Belfast stockbroker, by his wife Barbara, née Williamson.

His intense interest in drama and the theatre began when as a boy he met members of the original Ulster Theatre. At the Queen's University he took an honours degree in English Literature and became a leading member of the University Dramatic Society. It was the custom on the final night of a show to have a stage supper when each member of the cast was called upon to do a turn. Thus in 1926 he composed and recited *The Ballad of William Bloat*. It was conceived as a piece of fun with no political significance whatsoever. His ballad owes its appeal to the same kind of humour one finds in *The Drone* or *Thompson of Tir na n'Og*. The razor blade and the sheet are juxtaposed because of their strength; different kinds of strength but therein lies the wit. In the era of the electric razor or no razor at all it is hard to remember the evolution from the 'cut-throat' to the 'safety' blade in general use in the Twenties.

Now the ballad has passed into the folk memory of the Ulster people at home and abroad. There are many corrupt versions even though the original was published in the author's lifetime in an anthology of Ulster wit and humour entitled *Brave Crack!*. I am glad, therefore, to give permission for The Blackstaff Press to publish the authentic version. The illustrations by Hector McDonnell, an artist already acclaimed for his interpretation of realism and reality have their own intrinsic value though they may be as far from the author's intention as Belfast in 1982 differs from life there in 1926.

Irene Calvert
August 1982

I learned this poem from a cousin of mine, about 1970. It appealed to me because it seemed to encapsulate in miniature the tragedy of Belfast. It describes the pathetic and sometimes ludicrous consequences of violence through an absurd husband and wife quarrel. Not only that but it is an epitome of Belfast humour, which centres so often around hen-pecked husbands and family squabbles in mean streets.

I had for a long time been wanting to produce some work which would express my feelings about Belfast, and I decided that illustrating this bawdy parody was by far the most effective way of doing so. Almost inevitably anything which deals with violence in the city on a grander scale fails because it becomes moralising, and because it becomes impossible to express the rough humour and violent absurdity of life in Belfast.

Hector McDonnell

British Library Cataloguing in Publication Data

McDonnell, Hector
  The ballad of William Bloat.
  1. McDonnell, Hector   2. Etching – Northern Ireland
  I. Title   II. Calvert, Raymond
  769.92'4   NE2046.5.M/

  ISBN 0-85640-273-7

First published in 1982
by The Blackstaff Press Limited
3 Galway Park, Dundonald, Belfast BT16 0AN
with the assistance of the Arts Council
of Northern Ireland.

Printed in Northern Ireland by W.&G. Baird Limited